Travel G Valencia 2023

Discover the rich culture and vibrant flavour of Valencia

Scott O. Cortes

Copyright ©2023,Scott O. Cortes
All rights reserved. No part of this publication may be reproduced, stored in a retrieval system or transmitted in any form or by any means, electronic, mechanical, photocopying, recording or otherwise without prior written permission of the author, expect in the case of brief quotations embodied in critical reviews and certain other noncommercial uses permitted by copyright law.

Table Of Content

INTRODUCTION

VALENCIA'S CULTURAL HERITAGE

MUST-SEE LANDMARKS AND MONUMENTS

VALENCIA'S ART SCENE

VALENCIA'S VIBRANT CUISINE

EXPLORING VALENCIA'S OLD TOWN

VALENCIA'S NATURAL BEAUTY

VALENCIA'S MOUNTAINS AND HIKING TRAILS

BEYOND VALENCIA: DAY TRIPS AND EXCURSIONS

PRACTICAL INFORMATION FOR TRAVELLERS

USEFUL PHRASES

CONCLUSION

FINAL THOUGHTS ON VALENCIA

INTRODUCTION

Thank you for visiting "Travel Guide to Valencia 2023: Discover the Rich Culture and Vibrant Flavors of Valencia." This guidebook is intended to provide you all the knowledge you require to enjoy your visit to this stunning and culturally diverse city.

Every kind of traveller can find something to like in Valencia. Valencia has something for everyone, whether they are interested in nature, outdoor activities, food and wine, art and architecture, or history and culture. Valencia is one of the most well-liked tourist attractions in Spain due to its energetic street life, gorgeous beaches, and spectacular architecture.

Valencia's art, architecture, and festivals all represent the city's rich cultural legacy. The history of the city is lengthy and fascinating, going all the way back to the Roman era. Due to its advantageous location on the Mediterranean coast, it served as a major commerce hub and a cultural crucible for numerous civilizations over the millennia.

In the Middle Ages, Valencia was also home to a significant Islamic kingdom, which had a profound impact on the city's culture and architecture. The most well-known festival in Valencia, Las Fallas, honours the distinctive cultural identity of the city and is regarded as one of the most stunning celebrations in the entire globe.

Valencia is renowned for its distinctive cuisine, which combines Spanish and Mediterranean flavours. Paella is a rice dish that originated in Valencia and is now loved all over the world, and the city is well known for it. However, paella is not the only dish served in Valencia.

Fresh fruits, vegetables, and seafood are readily available in the city's markets, and there are numerous eateries and bars where you may sample regional specialties.

Valencia is a city that is simple to navigate on foot, and exploring its winding streets and alleyways is the best way to get a feel for it. Some of the most significant landmarks and monuments in Valencia can be found in its Old Town, one of Europe's largest and best-preserved historic centres. Among the must-see attractions of Valencia's Old Town are the Central Market, the Cathedral of Valencia, and the Lonja de la Seda (Silk Exchange).

Additionally, Valencia is surrounded by scenic landscapes like beaches, mountains, and parks. The city's beaches are some of the most well-liked in all of Spain, and they provide a variety of activities, including swimming, water sports, beach volleyball, and sunbathing. There are numerous parks and gardens where you may unwind and take in the city's natural beauty, as well as popular hiking and mountain bike trails in the mountains surrounding Valencia.

We will give you all the information you need to organise your trip to Valencia in this guidebook. We will discuss the natural beauty, the city's neighbourhoods and landmarks, its history and culture, and its gastronomy. Additionally, we will offer useful details on how to get to Valencia, how to navigate the area, and where to stay.

This manual is broken into six chapters. The cultural legacy of Valencia as well as its most significant landmarks and monuments are briefly described in Chapter 1. The colourful gastronomy of Valencia is examined in Chapter 2 along with some of the city's top dining establishments. The Old Town of Valencia, including its areas, famous buildings, and historic places, is the subject of Chapter 3.

The natural splendour of Valencia, including its beaches, mountains, and parks, is the subject of Chapter 4. Chapter 5 makes recommendations for day trips and excursions from Valencia, including journeys to Sagunto and the Albufera Natural Park. Finally, Chapter 6 offers useful advice for visitors, such as directions for getting to Valencia, how to navigate the city, where to stay, and how to keep safe.

This travel guide is intended to both encourage you to visit Valencia and to assist you in making the most of your time there.

VALENCIA'S CULTURAL HERITAGE

Valencia is a city with a lengthy and incredibly rich cultural legacy. The city has been inhabited since prehistoric times, and throughout history, it has served as a significant hub for trade and culture thanks to its advantageous location on the Mediterranean coast.

In 138 BC, the Romans established Valencia as a colony, and their influence can still be seen in the city's urban planning and architecture. The Almoina Archaeological Center, which houses the remnants of a Roman forum and other historic buildings, is one of Valencia's most remarkable specimens of Roman architecture.

Valencia was known as Medina al-Turab throughout the Middle Ages when it was a part of the Islamic Al-Andalus.

Valencia's culture and architecture were profoundly influenced by the Islamic era, as evidenced by the city's winding avenues, arches, and ornamental details. The Almudin, a storehouse and grain market from the 14th century, is the most well-known example of Islamic architecture in Valencia.

After being liberated from the Moors in 1238 by King James I of Aragon, Valencia officially entered the Christian era. The construction of the Cathedral of Valencia, one of the most notable landmarks in the city, and other significant improvements to Valencia's culture and architecture occurred throughout the Christian era.

The Gothic masterpiece cathedral is home to numerous priceless works of art, including a chalice that many people believe to be the Holy Grail. Valencia's festivals and customs are also examples of its cultural history. The annual Las

Fallas celebration, which takes place in March, is one of Valencia's most well-known events. Large paper-mâché and wood sculptures are built and burned as part of Las Fallas, a festival honouring the city's history and identity.

Numerous museums and galleries that highlight the city's cultural heritage are also located in Valencia. One of the most significant art museums in Spain is the Museum of Fine Arts of Valencia, which is home to a sizable collection of works of art dating from the Middle Ages to the present. Another significant museum that emphasises modern and contemporary art and design is the Valencian Institute of Modern Art (IVAM).

Valencia is renowned for its music and dance traditions in addition to its historical and aesthetic heritage. The jota, a traditional dance and music form that has its roots in the Aragon region, is one of the most well-liked musical subgenres in Valencia. The jota, which is frequently performed at festivals and other events, is distinguished by its vivacious rhythms and vibrant costumes.

Valencia's rich cultural past is a source of pride for its citizens and one of the main draws for the city's annual influx of millions of visitors. Valencia has much to offer for every kind of traveller, regardless of your interests in tradition, history, art, music, or any other of these things. You may learn more about Valencia's history and culture to better grasp who it is and where it fits in the world.

Valencia Historical Significance

Valencia has made an important contribution to the history of both Spain and the Mediterranean. For thousands of years, its strategic location on the eastern coast of the Iberian Peninsula has made it a centre for trade and cultural interchange.

With evidence of early human habitation dating to the Neolithic era, Valencia's history may be traced back to prehistoric times.

But the Roman conquest in 138 BC marked the start of the city's first history that has been documented. Valentia Edetanorum, a flourishing colony founded by the Romans in Valencia, rose to prominence as a major hub for trade and agriculture. Valencia's architecture and urban design are still influenced by the Roman era.

Valencia was ruled by the Visigoths and then the Moors following the fall of the Roman Empire. Valencia, then known as Medina al-Turab, flourished as a centre of learning and culture during the Islamic era, drawing intellectuals and creatives from all over the Muslim world. Valencia's culture and architecture were profoundly influenced by the Islamic era, as evidenced by the city's winding avenues, arches, and ornamental details.

The Christian era in Valencia's history began with King James I of Aragon's conquest of Valencia in 1238. Valencia's culture and architecture saw enormous transformations during the Christian era, including the building of the Cathedral of Valencia, one of the city's most notable landmarks. A chalice that is thought to be the Holy Grail is among the priceless items of art that are kept in the Gothic masterpiece that is the Cathedral.

The Spanish Golden Age, which took place between the 16th and 17th centuries and saw significant artistic and economic development in Spain, was greatly influenced by Valencia.

Many of Valencia's most stunning structures and monuments were constructed during this period, and the city developed into a centre for the production of silk, which was highly prized throughout Europe. One of the most remarkable specimens of Valencian Gothic architecture, The Silk Exchange, or La Lonja de la Seda, has been recognized as a UNESCO World Heritage Site.

Valencia saw substantial growth and modernization during the 20th century. Both Republican and Nationalist forces fought for control of the city during the Spanish Civil War, and the city played a significant part in the conflict. Following the war, Valencia experienced a period of economic and social change during which the city's landscape was drastically altered by rapid urbanisation and industrialization.

Valencia is a thriving, dynamic city today that blends its rich historical past with contemporary innovation and creativity.

It is a fascinating location for history historians and culture aficionados alike due to its historical significance, which is reflected in its numerous landmarks, museums, and cultural events. Visitors can better comprehend Valencia's identity and role in the world by learning more about the city's past.

MUST-SEE LANDMARKS AND MONUMENTS

Many breathtaking monuments and landmarks can be found in Valencia, which is known for its vibrant history and culture. There are numerous must-see attractions in Valencia, including modernist and Gothic cathedrals. Some of the most popular sites to see are listed below:

- One of the most significant landmarks in the city is the magnificent Gothic cathedral in Valencia. Its style is a fusion of Gothic, Baroque, and Romanesque, and it is the location of the Holy Grail.

- Several cultural and scientific organisations, including an opera theatre, a science museum, and an aquarium, are housed in the modernist complex known as The City of Arts and Sciences.

- **La Lonja de la Seda:** This magnificent specimen of Valencian Gothic architecture is a UNESCO World Heritage Site. It was formerly a hub for the silk trade and is now a museum that highlights the vibrant cultural history of the city.

- **Torres de Serranos:** Valencia's former main entrance was one of these majestic Gothic towers. They are a well-liked location for both tourists and locals nowadays because they provide breathtaking views of the city.

- One of the biggest markets in Europe is Mercado Central, where a vast variety of food and drink vendors can be found. It is a fantastic location to try some of

Valencia's well-known dishes, such as paella and horchata.

- Just outside the city is the breathtaking Albufera Natural Park, which has a sizable lake and a wide diversity of plants and animals. It's a perfect location to get away from the city's noise and enjoy some peace in the outdoors.

- **Plaza de la Virgen:** In the core of Valencia's historic district, this charming square is home to a blend of Gothic, Baroque, and Romanesque buildings. It's a terrific spot to take in the energy of the city while sipping coffee or enjoying a snack at one of the surrounding cafes.

- The Silk Museum is a museum that highlights Valencia's rich silk heritage and houses a variety of exhibits and relics associated with the silk industry. It is situated in the Velluters old neighbourhood.

- One of the most recognizable structures in the city is the Central Post Office, a beautiful modernist structure created by Valencia-born architect Miguel Angel Navarro. It is centrally positioned in the city and a popular spot for selfies and photos.

- The Valencia Bioparc is a zoo where a variety of creatures live, including tigers, gorillas, and elephants. It is renowned for its cutting-edge style and emphasis on education and conservation.

These are only a few of Valencia's numerous sights and monuments. In this dynamic and interesting city, there is something for everyone, regardless of your interests in history, architecture, or nature.

VALENCIA'S ART SCENE

Valencia is a city with a thriving modern art scene and a rich cultural history. There are many ways to enjoy Valencia's art scene, from breathtaking museums to cutting-edge galleries. The following are a few of Valencia's top art destinations:

- One of the most significant modern art museums in Spain is IVAM (Institut Valencià d'Art Modern), which houses a wide variety of current works by Spanish and foreign artists. The collection includes creations by artists such as Yoko Ono, Joan Miró, and Antoni Tàpies.

- Spanish art from the Gothic and Renaissance eras to modern art can be found in the Museo de Bellas Artes de Valencia. Famous

Spanish artists like Francisco Goya and Joaquin Sorolla have pieces in the collection.

- One of Valencia's most significant contemporary art galleries, Galera Espai Tactel exhibits the work of up-and-coming artists from both Spain and beyond. The gallery is renowned for its cutting-edge exhibits and dedication to helping emerging artists.

- **La Nave:** This contemporary art centre offers a variety of exhibits, concerts, and events. It is situated in the hip Ruzafa area. The location is devoted to fostering modern art and culture in Valencia and is administered by a group of artists.

- Sala Parpalló is a modern art gallery with a variety of exhibitions and activities that highlight cutting-edge work by both regional and international artists. It is situated in Valencia's old centre.

- The Institut Français de Valencia is a cultural institution that promotes French culture in Valencia by hosting a variety of exhibitions, performances, and other activities that are connected to French art and culture.

- **Galera Luis Adelantado:** One of Valencia's oldest galleries of modern art, noted for promoting up-and-coming and mid-career artists. A variety of artistic disciplines, such as painting, sculpture, and installation art, are on display in the gallery.

- **Centro del Carmen:** This cultural hub offers a variety of exhibits, performances, and events and is housed in a former convent in the middle of Valencia's historic district. The centre showcases both established and up-and-coming artists' work and is dedicated to fostering modern art and culture.

- Espai Rambleta is a diverse cultural hub that offers a variety of exhibitions, concerts, and events in the fields of art, music, theatre, and film. It is situated in the San Marcelino area.

- Located in a former factory, Bombas Gens is a contemporary art venue that hosts a variety of shows, activities, and performances focused on modern and contemporary art and culture. The gallery is one of Valencia's most cutting-edge art locations and is devoted to fostering social and cultural transformation via art.

These are just a few of Valencia's many locations where you can find art. There is something for everyone in Valencia's vibrant and diversified art scene, whether you are interested in modern art or traditional Spanish art.

VALENCIA'S VIBRANT CUISINE

Spain's Valencia region is well known for its vibrant and varied food, which is influenced by the area's rich cultural past, Mediterranean climate, and closeness to the sea.

The culinary scene of Valencia is renowned for its use of local, fresh products, strong flavours, and traditional cooking methods. When visiting Valencia, try these recommended dishes and culinary experiences:

- Paella is a rice-based dish that is frequently prepared with chicken, rabbit, or shellfish and is seasoned with saffron, garlic, and paprika. It is arguably the most well-known cuisine to come from Valencia. Traditional paella is prepared in a sizable, shallow pan over an open flame and is accompanied by a side of alioli (garlic mayonnaise).

- **Fideuà:** A Valencian dish made with noodles that is similar to paella. Thin noodles are used to make fideuà instead of rice, and shrimp, mussels, and squid are frequently included.

- Eel is cooked in a broth of potatoes, potatoes, garlic, and paprika in the classic Valencian cuisine known as All i Pebre. For dipping, crusty bread is frequently provided with the entrée.

- Horchata is a popular beverage in Valencia, especially in the sweltering summer months. It is made from tiger nuts, sugar, and water. Cold horchata is frequently served, and fartons, a sweet pastry, are frequently served alongside it.

- A famous beverage in Valencia's pubs and clubs is the "Agua de Valencia," a concoction of orange juice, cava (Spanish sparkling wine), gin, and vodka.

- **Turrón:** Made from honey, sugar, and almonds, this delicious treat is a variety of nougat. In Valencia, turrón is a well-liked delicacy, especially around the holidays.

- The well-known street snack known as a bocadillo de Calamares consists of a crusty baguette stuffed with deep-fried squid rings and a dollop of alioli.

- **Arroz al Horno:** Made with pork ribs, sausages, and chickpeas, this hearty dish is a baked rice casserole. The recipe is a favourite throughout the winter because of its saffron, paprika, and garlic flavours.

- **Churros with Chocolate:** A cup of rich, hot chocolate is served alongside deep-fried churros in this traditional Spanish treat.

- **Mercado Central:** For foodies, Valencia's lively food market in the city's historic centre is a must-see location. The market has a large selection of stalls providing baked goods, fresh produce, fish, meats, and cheeses.

Valencia's cuisine reflects the city's diverse historical and cultural influences, from the Arabic spices that are used in many dishes to the local Mediterranean seafood that is always fresh. Valencia's diverse culinary culture is likely to satisfy your palate, whether you prefer more experimental food or traditional Spanish meals.

Introduction to Valencia Cuisine

The rich cultural heritage, distinctive topography, and close proximity to the Mediterranean Sea are all reflected in the dynamic and varied culinary tradition known as Valencian cuisine.

Valencia, a region in eastern Spain, is renowned for its vast coastline, abundant agriculture, and warm, sunny atmosphere, all of which contribute to the region's outstanding cuisine.

The history of the area, which has been formed by centuries of cultural and culinary influences, serves as the source of inspiration for Valencian cuisine. The Moors, who dominated the area for more than 500 years, brought a variety of spices and culinary methods that are still used in the region's cuisine today. Valencia has additionally benefited from being a hub for trade and migration due to its location on the Mediterranean Sea, which has led to a wide variety of cultural and gastronomic influences over the years.

Paella, a savoury rice dish that has come to be associated with Spanish cuisine, is one of the most recognizable dishes of Valencian cuisine.

The meal is traditionally prepared in a big, shallow skillet over an open flame and made with saffron, paprika, and a variety of meats or shellfish. Other well-liked foods include all i pebre, a hearty eel stew, and fideuà, a similar dish served with thin noodles rather than rice.

Valencia is renowned for its sweet delicacies as well, including turrón, a form of nougat made with honey and almonds, and horchata, a cool beverage made from tiger nuts. The markets in the area, like the well-known Mercado Central in Valencia's old town, sell a variety of fresh fruits, vegetables, fish, meats, cheeses, and baked items.

Chefs and food enthusiasts alike are praising the distinctive flavours and culinary traditions of the Valencian region as Valencian cuisine has recently undergone a comeback in popularity. Valencia's culinary sector is certain to develop and excite the senses as more tourists learn about its gastronomic treasures.

Traditional Dishes and Drinks

Traditional foods and beverages are abundant in Valencia and are adored by both locals and visitors. Here are some of the most well-known:

- **Paella:** It is impossible to talk about Valencian food without bringing up paella. Usually made with saffron, paprika, and a variety of meats or seafood, this savoury rice meal is prepared in a big, shallow pan and cooked over an open flame. Paella comes in many forms, but the most conventional is made using chicken and rabbit.

- **Fideuà:** A dish similar to paella that uses thin noodles rather than rice. Although there are versions that also include meat or vegetables, seafood is the most common ingredient in this preparation.

- **All I pebre:** A typical meal from the Albufera region near Valencia is this garlicky eel stew. Typically, eel, potatoes, garlic, and several other spices are used to make it.

- Known as "oven-baked rice," arroz al horno is a filling casserole consisting of rice, pig ribs, sausage, and beans.

- **Horchata:** Made from tiger nuts, this cool beverage is a favourite during sweltering summer days. It is frequently served over ice and has a sweet, nutty flavour.

- Orange juice, cava (Spanish sparkling wine), vodka, and gin are the main ingredients in the neighbourhood's favourite cocktail known as Agua de Valencia. It is frequently shared among friends and served in a sizable pitcher.

- **Turrón:** Made commonly in Valencia with honey, almonds, and sugar, this nougat is a beloved sweet treat. Turrón comes in two primary varieties: soft turrón, which is more fudge-like in texture, and hard turrón, which is crunchy and may be eaten like a candy bar.

These foods and beverages are just a small sample of Valencia's diverse culinary heritage. Valencia has much to offer everyone, whether you're a foodie eager to discover the regional cuisine or just searching for a filling and delectable lunch.

Best Places to eat in Valencia

Valencia has a thriving food scene, with a large selection of eateries, cafes, and markets serving a wide variety of foods. The following are some of Valencia's top restaurants:

- The classic paella served at Casa Carmela, a famous eatery in Valencia's Cabanyal neighbourhood along the city's shore, is famous for being prepared over an open flame and accompanied by a side of aioli (a garlicky mayonnaise).

- **La Pepica:** La Pepica, another well-known paella restaurant, has been serving the well-known rice dish since 1898. This eatery, which can be found on Valencia's coastal promenade, is popular among both locals and tourists.

- For foodies, the Mercado Central in Valencia's historic centre is a must-see. There is something for everyone here with over 1,000 stalls providing fresh fruit, meats, fish, and baked goodies. For some of the best tapas in the city, make sure to visit Central Bar, which is housed inside the market.

- Chef Ricard Camarena is one of Valencia's most renowned culinary artists and owns several restaurants there. His self-named eatery is a fine-dining establishment that serves a tasting menu that highlights the local flavours and delicacies.

- La Riua is a charming restaurant serving typical Valencian food. It is situated in Valencia's historic district. A few of the menu items at

the restaurant are all I pebre, fideuà, and arroz al horno.
- La Pilareta is a popular spot among people in Valencia's El Carmen district. The bar's boquerones (marinated anchovies), which come with a side of potato chips, are its specialty.
- **Lienzo:** This cutting-edge eatery in Valencia's hip Ruzafa area serves inventive, modern interpretations of regional specialties. The menu is periodically updated to highlight the best seasonal ingredients.
- Valencia offers much to offer for every taste and price range, whether you're seeking traditional paella or cutting-edge, modern cuisine. Discover some of the hidden gems that make Valencia one of Spain's top culinary destinations by exploring the city's culinary scene.

EXPLORING VALENCIA'S OLD TOWN

The Old Town of Valencia, also called Ciutat Vella, is a picturesque and ancient district that is ideal for strolling through. Here are some of the top places to see and things to do in this energetic area of the city:

- The Cathedral of Valencia, the Basilica of the Virgin of the Helpless, and the Palace of the Generalitat may all be found on Valencia's Plaza de la Virgen, one of the city's most popular gathering spots.

- With over 1,000 kiosks selling everything from fresh produce to regional cheeses and cured meats, the Central Market is a food lover's heaven. For some of the best tapas in the area, make sure to visit Central Bar.

- The Gothic-style Lonja de la Seda structure, which formerly housed the city's silk trade, has been designated a UNESCO World Heritage Site. The Sala de Contratación, the main hall of the structure, is a magnificent illustration of Valencian Gothic design.

- The Torres de Serranos provide sweeping views of Valencia's historic district and were previously a part of the city's defensive walls. The towers' summits are accessible to visitors for a modest price.

- The best pubs, cafes, and restaurants in Valencia can be found in the trendy Barrio del Carmen, which is also home to several art galleries and cultural institutions.

- The remarkable collection of paintings and sculptures at Museo de Bellas Artes, one of Spain's top art museums, includes pieces by Goya, Velázquez, and Sorolla.

- **Plaza Redonda:** Shops selling typical Valencian crafts and trinkets, including fans, espadrilles, and pottery, may be found in this unusual circular area.

- **Mercado de Colon:** This former market structure has been renovated into a posh dining and shopping locale with several eateries, cafes, and boutiques.

- The Old Town of Valencia has something to offer everyone, regardless of their interests in history, art, or cuisine. Take your time strolling through this attractive area and taking in the diverse cultural traditions of the city.

Getting to know Valencia's Old Town

Valencia's Old Town, or Ciutat Vella, is a lively and storied district that is brimming with charm and personality. Here are some pointers for exploring this stunning area of the city:

- **Take a walking tour:** Exploring Valencia's Old Town on foot is one of the best ways to do so. You may gain your bearings and learn about the neighbourhood's history and culture by taking one of the many guided walking tours offered by local businesses.

- **Visit the landmarks:** The Cathedral of Valencia, the Central Market, and the Lonja de la Seda are just a few of the significant structures that can be found in Valencia's Old Town. Spend some time visiting these famous locations and learning about their significance and history.

- **Discover the streets and alleys:** The Old Town of Valencia is full of small, interesting streets and passageways. Take a stroll through the area to find secret plazas, quaint cafes, and quaint shops.

- **Try the food:** Some of Valencia's top eateries, cafes, and bars are located in the Old Town. Don't forget to try some of the regional food, which includes classic dishes like paella and fideuà.

- **Attend a cultural event:** Valencia's Old Town serves as a centre for the arts, hosting several festivals, concerts, and shows all year long. To sample the thriving local arts scene, check the listings and go to an event.

- **Visit the museums:** The Museum of Fine Arts and the Valencian Museum of Ethnology are two of the museums located in Valencia's Old Town. Spend some time looking around these places to discover Valencia's diverse cultural legacy.

- **Buy souvenirs:** Valencia's Old Town is a fantastic location to buy presents and souvenirs. Buy traditional Valencian crafts like fans and ceramics at the Plaza Redonda, or look for one-of-a-kind items by browsing the local boutiques and shops.

Anyone visiting Valencia should make a point of visiting the Old Town, which is a must-see location whether you're interested in history, culture, or cuisine. Spend some time getting to know this lovely area and all that it has to offer.

Must-See Sites in Valencia's Old Town

The Old Town, or Ciutat Vella, of Valencia, is a quaint and distinguished district with a wealth of fascinating landmarks and attractions. Some of the attractions you simply must see while you're here are listed below:

- The Holy Chalice, which is believed to be the cup that Jesus drank from at the Last Supper, is kept in the Cathedral of Valencia, a striking Gothic structure that dates to the 13th century.

- With over 1,000 kiosks selling everything from fresh produce to regional cheeses and cured meats, the Central Market is a food lover's heaven. For some of the best tapas in the area, make sure to visit Central Bar.

- The Gothic-style Lonja de la Seda, formerly the city's silk exchange, is now a UNESCO World Heritage Site. The Sala de Contratación, the main hall of the structure, is a magnificent illustration of Valencian Gothic design.

- The Torres de Serranos provide sweeping views of Valencia's historic district and were previously a part of the city's defensive walls. The towers' summits are accessible to visitors for a modest price.

- The Basilica of the Virgin of the Helpless and the Palace of the Generalitat are two significant landmarks that may be found in Valencia's Plaza de la Virgen, one of the city's most popular gathering spots.

- The best pubs, cafes, and restaurants in Valencia can be found in the trendy Barrio del Carmen, which is also home to several art galleries and cultural institutions.

- The Museum of Fine Arts is one of Spain's top art museums and is home to a significant collection of sculptures and paintings, including creations by Goya, Velázquez, and Sorolla.

- The Plaza Redonda is a distinctive circular area where several stores provide typical Valencian handicrafts and mementos like fans, espadrilles, and pottery.

- The Mercado de Colon is a former market structure that has been converted into a fashionable dining and retail district with several eateries, cafes, and boutiques.

The Old Town of Valencia has something to offer everyone, regardless of their interests in history, art, or cuisine. Take your time and explore this charming neighbourhood to find all of its hidden treasures.

Valencia Old Town Neighbourhoods

The Old Town of Valencia is separated into several distinct neighbourhoods, each having its particular personality and attractions. The following are a few of the most intriguing areas to visit:

- **El Carmen:** There's a good reason why this area of Valencia's Old Town is possibly the most well-known. Some of the best pubs, cafes, and restaurants in the city can be found in El Carmen, a neighbourhood full of tiny lanes and old buildings. Additionally, it's a great location to buy souvenirs and local crafts.

- **La Seu:** This area is home to several significant structures, including the Palace of the Generalitat and the Basilica of the Virgin of the Helpless, and is centred around the city's magnificent Gothic cathedral. The area around the cathedral is teeming with stores and cafes, and at night, street performers and musicians bring the neighbourhood to life.

- **El Mercat:** The Central Market, one of Valencia's most well-known attractions, is the focal point of this area. The market's surrounding streets are teeming with bustling bars and cafes, and it's a terrific spot to try regional food and shop for fresh goods.

- **El Pilar:** Many of the stunning Art Nouveau structures in this area date from the first half of the 20th century. The Basilica of the Virgin of the Forsaken and the Valencian Museum of Ethnology are two additional significant landmarks in the area.

- **The Valencia Botanical Gardens,** which span more than 8 hectares and house thousands of plant species from all over the world, are located in the El Botanic area. The gardens are a tranquil haven in the middle of the city and a wonderful spot to unwind.

- **La Xerea:** This area, which is immediately south of La Seu, is home to several historic structures and sites, including the Museum of Fine Arts and the Palace of the Marqués de Dos Aguas. The region is renowned for its high-end stores and boutiques.

- **El Arrabal:** This area, which is just outside the ancient city walls, is renowned for its buzzing atmosphere and active nightlife. It's a terrific location for dancing the night away or getting a few beers.

Valencia's Old Town neighbourhoods have something to offer for everyone, whether you're interested in history, architecture, or simply soaking up the local culture. To properly enjoy these communities' beauty and uniqueness, be sure to stroll around them.

VALENCIA'S NATURAL BEAUTY

Valencia is renowned for its gorgeous architecture, vibrant food, and extensive cultural heritage in addition to its stunning natural surroundings. The city has several parks, gardens, and beaches, and it is surrounded by stunning natural scenery. You shouldn't skip any of these Valencia natural attractions:

- One of Spain's biggest urban parks, Turia Gardens, runs for more than 9 kilometres from the City of Arts and Sciences to the Bioparc.

  It was once the Turia River's riverbed before a disastrous flood caused it to be diverted outside of the city. The park is ideal for outdoor activities like riding, walking, and jogging. Numerous playgrounds, sports facilities, and cultural venues are also located there.

- **Albufera Natural Park** is a designated wetland region south of Valencia that is well-known for its rice fields and breathtaking sunsets. You may go birdwatching, take a boat trip on the Albufera lake, or just unwind on the beach. There are also various traditional eateries in the park where you may sample regional rice specialties.

- **La Calderona Natural Park** is a mountain area just to the north of Valencia that is great for horseback riding, cycling, and hiking. Numerous trails in the park provide breathtaking views of the Mediterranean Sea in addition to a wide range of flora and fauna.

- **Saler Beach,** which is situated in the Albufera Natural Park, is one of Valencia's most stunning beaches. Swimmable, sun-kissed, and restful, the beach is renowned for its crystal-clear waters and fine sand.

- **Cabecera Park** is a sizable park in Valencia's northwest that's great for strolling, picnicking, and cycling. The park is the location of the Bioparc Valencia, a zoo that specialises in African species, as well as a number of man-made lakes, gardens, and playgrounds.

- **The Jardines de Monforte** is a stunning garden in the centre of Valencia that is well-known for its exotic flora and water features. The garden, which was created in the 19th century, is ideal for a quiet stroll or a special date.

Valencia's natural beauty will enchant you whether you enjoy outdoor activities or simply want to get away from the city's noise and bustle. Spend some time exploring these natural wonders and taking in the breathtaking scenery that surrounds the city.

Valencia Beaches and Coastline

The coastline of Valencia is renowned for its gorgeous beaches, crystal-clear waters, and balmy weather. Valencia's beaches have something to offer everyone, whether you're looking for a quiet getaway or an exciting day out. Some of Valencia's top beaches are listed below:

- The most well-known beach in Valencia is Malvarrosa Beach, which is situated close to the port.

  The beach is well-liked by both locals and visitors and provides a variety of amenities like showers, sun loungers, and beach bars. The promenade is surrounded by eateries and coffee shops, making it the ideal location for a day by the sea.

- **El Saler Beach,** which is situated in the Albufera Natural Park, is one of Valencia's most stunning beaches. The beach is popular for its dunes and its clean seas, making it the ideal place for swimming, tanning, and water sports.

- **Pinedo Beach** is a peaceful, undeveloped beach that is close to Valencia. The beach is the ideal location for a leisurely day out because of its tranquil atmosphere and reputation for having golden sand.

- **North of Valencia,** in a charming area famed for its colourful homes and little marina, lies Port Saplaya Beach. Due to its variety of amenities, which include a playground and a beach volleyball court, the beach is excellent for families with young children.

- **La Garrofera Beach** is a remote beach in Valencia's north that is renowned for its pristine surroundings and natural beauty. For those looking to get away from the throng and spend a quiet day by the water, the beach is ideal.

- Along with these beaches, Valencia's coastline has a number of rocky bays and coves that are ideal for diving and snorkelling.

The Cabo de la Huerta, the Isla de Tabarca, and the Cala del Racó del Corb are a few of the best locations. Valencia's beaches and shoreline have something to offer everyone, whether you're searching for a fun day out or a quiet place to unwind.

VALENCIA'S MOUNTAINS AND HIKING TRAILS

Valencia has stunning mountains and hiking paths, so its natural beauty goes beyond its beaches and shoreline. The following are some of the top locations to explore the mountains and hiking trails in Valencia:

- The Sierra de Espadán is a mountain range in the north of Valencia that is renowned for its breathtaking scenery and plethora of animals.

    There are many hiking trails throughout the range, from simple strolls to strenuous excursions. The Font de la Salut, the Mas del Frare, and the Penyagolosa Peak are a few of the Sierra de Espadán's features.

- The small village of Montanejos, which is situated in the Castellón mountains, is well-known for its picturesque surroundings and its natural hot springs. The town has several hiking paths, including the Cascada del Estrecho and the Barranco de la Maimona, and is surrounded by mountains.

- Calderona Natural Park is a well-known park with stunning scenery and a wide variety of fauna that is situated in the mountains halfway between Valencia and Castellón.

There are many hiking trails in the park, from simple strolls to more difficult hikes. Garb Peak, the Ojos Negros Greenway, and the Les Rodanes Ravine are a few of the features of the Calderona Natural Park.

- On the coast of Alicante, there is a natural park called Serra Gelada, which is renowned for its craggy cliffs and breathtaking coastal scenery. The Faro de el Albir and the Mirador dels Bandolers are only two of the park's many hiking trails.

- Natural park Alto Turia, which is situated in Valencia's mountains, is renowned for its breathtaking vistas and plethora of species. There are many hiking trails in the park, from simple strolls to more difficult hikes. The Pico del Ropé and the Charcos del Ral are two of the attractions of the Alto Turia Natural Park.

- Valencia's mountains and hiking routes have plenty to offer everyone, whether you're a seasoned hiker or simply seeking a stroll. Exploring Valencia's mountains and hiking trails is a life-changing experience because of the region's breathtaking scenery, abundant animals, and breathtaking views.

Valencia Parks and Gardens

Valencia is a city that cherishes nature, and as a result, it has a lot of parks and gardens that offer a haven of greenery amidst the concrete jungle. The top parks and gardens in Valencia are listed below:

- **Jardines del Real,** also referred to as the Royal Gardens, is a sizable park that spans more than 100,000 square metres. It has a sizable lake, numerous fountains, and a diversity of different trees and plants. Visitors to the park can unwind on any of the many benches or explore the many walks and trails.

- **Turia Gardens:** This park was created on the site where the Turia River had flowed before it was diverted due to flooding. The park is more than nine kilometres long and has a variety of attractions, such as playgrounds, athletic fields, and gardens. It's a well-liked location for walking, cycling, and jogging.

- **Cabecera Park** is a sizable park with several lakes, an aviary, and a rose garden that is situated alongside the Turia River. It's a wonderful location for a picnic or a calm stroll.

- **The Monforte Gardens,** which are in the centre of Valencia's historic district, are renowned for their exquisite landscaping and elaborate fountains. Early in the 20th century, the gardens—which had previously been the private grounds of a wealthy family—were made public.

- **Albufera Natural Park** is a park with a sizable freshwater lake that is home to several bird and fish species. It is situated immediately south of Valencia. The lake can be toured by boat, or visitors can walk through the wetlands nearby.

- **Benicalap Park** is a sizable park that attracts plenty of families. It has a skate park, several playgrounds, and a sizable pond with ducks and geese.

The parks and gardens of Valencia provide a welcome escape from the bustle of the city. Valencia's parks and gardens provide something for everyone, whether you're searching for a peaceful location to read a book or a lively place to take the kids.

BEYOND VALENCIA: DAY TRIPS AND EXCURSIONS

Valencia has a lot to offer, but there are also a lot of interesting sites to visit nearby. Here are a few fantastic day trips and excursions to take into account:

- **Albufera** is a freshwater lake that is home to several bird and fish species. It is only a short drive south of Valencia. The lake can be toured by boat, or visitors can walk through the wetlands nearby.

- **Xàtiva** is a charming town with a mediaeval castle and a lovely old town that is about an hour's drive from Valencia. The castle offers breathtaking views of the surrounding countryside as it sits atop a hill overlooking the town.

- Approximately an hour's drive west of Valencia is the small town of Requena, which is well-known for its wine. The best wines from the area can be tasted when on a tour of the nearby wineries.

- One hour's drive inland from Valencia is the small community of Montanejos, which is well-known for its thermal springs. While relaxing in the hot springs, visitors can take in the breathtaking mountain scenery.

- **Peiscola:** A charming coastal town with a magnificent castle and a lovely old town, Peiscola is about two hours' drive north of Valencia. The renowned television series Game of Thrones uses the castle as a filming location.

- **Sagunto:** This historic town is close to Valencia by train and is well-known for its Roman ruins, which include an amphitheatre that has been maintained.

Within a short drive of Valencia, there is something for everyone, regardless of your interests in nature, history, or culture. These day trips and excursions are fantastic ways to explore the area more and take advantage of everything it has to offer.

ALBUFERA NATURAL PARK

Just south of Valencia is the lovely nature preserve known as Albufera Natural Park. It is renowned for having a sizable freshwater lake that supports a huge diversity of fish and birds. It is one of Spain's most significant wetlands and spans an area of more than 21,000 hectares.

The park at Albufera can be explored on foot, by bicycle, or by boat. Visitors get the opportunity to explore the park's rich animals up close on the several hiking and cycling routes that snake through the marshes. The lake itself is a well-liked location for birdwatching, boating, and fishing.

A tour of the lake by boat is one of the attractions of a trip to Albufera. Visitors can enjoy a leisurely ride aboard a "albuferenc," a classic flat-bottomed boat. The boat trips provide a wonderful opportunity to see some of the numerous bird species that call the lake home, including herons, egrets, and flamingos. They also offer a new perspective on the breathtaking nature of the park.

Albufera is well-known for its natural beauty as well as its rice fields. The park is home to some of Spain's best rice fields, and visitors can discover the age-old farming techniques that have been practised there.

Visitors to Albufera can experience some of the region's delectable rice dishes at one of the numerous nearby eateries because rice plays a significant role in Valencian cuisine.

Albufera Natural Park is a must-see location for environment enthusiasts and anyone curious about Valencian culture and food, in general. It is simple to understand why this park is one of the most well-liked tourist destinations in the Valencia region given its breathtaking beauty, diversified animals, and extensive history.

The Town of Sagunto

Just to the north of Valencia is the historic town of Sagunto. It is renowned for its beautiful ancient town and well-preserved Roman remains. Visitors to Sagunto may take in the tranquil ambiance of this picturesque location while exploring the town's numerous historic sites.

The Roman Theater is among Sarento's top attractions. One of the best preserved Roman theatres in Spain, this remarkable building is from the first century AD. Imagine what it must have been like to watch a play or performance here more than two thousand years ago as visitors go around the theatre.

The Castle is yet another important attraction in Sagunto. This fortress offers breathtaking views of the surrounding countryside as it towers above the town. The town's history has been significantly influenced by the castle, which was built in the ninth century.

Sagunto is home to several museums and art galleries in addition to its historical buildings. While the Palau de Betlem Museum features modern art and design, the Sagunto History Museum is a fantastic place to learn more about the town's fascinating history.

Sagunto has a wide variety of stores, eateries, and cafes for tourists to enjoy. The old town is very attractive, with winding streets and antique buildings that are pleasant to meander through. Naturally, no trip to Sagunto would be complete without trying some of the local cuisine, which is renowned for its fresh seafood and authentic rice dishes.

Sagunto is a fantastic day trip from Valencia since it allows visitors to travel back in time and see a fascinating period of Spanish history. Sagunto is guaranteed to be a highlight of any trip to the Valencia region with its historic ruins, a magnificent castle, and quaint old town.

More Day Trips from Valencia

Visitors can discover a variety of other fantastic day trip sites from Valencia in addition to Sagunto and Albufera Natural Park. Here are some recommendations:

- The picturesque town of Xàtiva, which is about an hour south of Valencia, is well-known for its imposing castle and ancient old town. Xàtiva, which contains a multitude of fascinating museums and galleries, has a significant place in Spanish history.

- **Cullera:** Visitors can unwind on the beach and take in the Mediterranean sun at this seaside town, which is about 45 minutes south of Valencia. A historic castle and other fascinating museums may be found in Cullera.

- **Pescola:** This lovely coastal town, which is about two hours drive from Valencia, is well-known for its magnificent castle and charming old town. Pescola is a well-liked tourist resort and has a long history that dates back to the Middle Ages.

- The picturesque village of Montanejos, which is about an hour and a half's drive north of Valencia, is well-known for its natural hot springs and stunning mountain landscape. Visitors can unwind in the hot springs or pedal their way through the surrounding countryside.

- About an hour's drive west of Valencia is the charming town of Requena, which is renowned for both its old town and winemaking. Along with several intriguing museums and galleries, Requena is home to several wineries that provide tours and tastings.

There are day trip destinations close to Valencia that are likely to fit your interests, whether you enjoy history, wildlife, or just lounging on the beach. It's understandable why the Valencia region is a well-liked travel destination for tourists to Spain with the abundance of fascinating and stunning locations to discover.

PRACTICAL INFORMATION FOR TRAVELLERS

Here is some practical information for travellers visiting Valencia:

- **Language:** The official language of Valencia is Spanish. English is widely spoken in tourist areas, but it's always helpful to learn a few basic Spanish phrases.

- **Currency:** The currency in Valencia is the Euro. Most places accept credit cards, but it's always good to have some cash on hand for smaller purchases.

- **Climate:** Valencia has a Mediterranean climate, with mild winters and hot summers. The best time to visit is in the spring or fall, when the weather is comfortable and there are fewer crowds.

- **Transportation:** Valencia has a good public transportation system, including buses, trams, and a metro system. Taxis are also readily available. Biking is also a popular way to get around, with many bike rental options available.

- **Accommodation:** Valencia has a wide range of accommodation options, including hotels, hostels, and vacation rentals. The most popular areas to stay are the old town and the beach areas.

- **Safety:** Valencia is a safe city, but it's always a good idea to take precautions against theft and pickpocketing, especially in crowded tourist areas.

- **Electricity:** Valencia uses 220 volts, with a European-style two-pin plug. Visitors from North America may need to bring a plug adapter.

- **Wi-Fi:** Wi-Fi is widely available in Valencia, with many cafes, restaurants, and public spaces offering free Wi-Fi.

- **Tipping:** Tipping is not a common practice in Valencia, but it's always appreciated for exceptional service.

- **Emergency numbers:** In case of emergency, dial 112 for general emergencies, 091 for the police, and 061 for medical emergencies.

With this information in mind, travellers to Valencia can enjoy a safe and enjoyable visit to this vibrant and fascinating city.

Getting to Valencia

Valencia is easily accessible by various modes of transportation. Here are some options for getting to Valencia:

- **Plane:** Valencia has its own international airport, Valencia Airport (VLC), which is located approximately 8 km from the city centre. It's a busy airport with many international and domestic flights, and it's well-connected to the city centre by metro, bus, and taxi.

- **Train:** Valencia has excellent train connections to other parts of Spain and Europe. The main train station is Estación del Norte, which is located in the city centre. There are high-speed trains (AVE) that connect Valencia with Madrid, Barcelona, and other major cities.

- **Bus:** There are many bus companies that operate in Valencia, connecting it with other cities in Spain and Europe. The main bus station is Estación de Autobuses de Valencia, which is located close to the city centre.

- **Car:** Valencia is well-connected by highways and motorways, making it easy to reach by car. However, driving in the city centre can be challenging, and parking can be difficult to find and expensive.

- **Ferry:** There are ferry services that connect Valencia with the Balearic Islands and other parts of Spain. The ferry terminal is located in the port area, close to the city centre.

Once in Valencia, getting around the city is easy with a good public transportation system that includes buses, trams, and a metro system. Biking is also a popular way to get around, with many bike rental options available. Taxis are also readily available.

Getting Around Valencia

Valencia has a well-developed public transportation system, making it easy to get around the city. Here are some options for getting around Valencia:

- **Metro:** Valencia's metro system is modern, efficient, and well-connected. It has six lines that cover the entire city and connect it with the suburbs. The metro runs from 5:30 am to midnight, and the frequency of trains is every 5-10 minutes.

- **Bus:** Valencia has an extensive bus network that covers the entire city and connects it with the suburbs. There are different types of buses, including regular buses, night buses, and tourist buses. The frequency of buses varies depending on the route, but they usually run from early morning until late at night.

- **Tram:** Valencia has two tram lines that connect the city centre with the coastal areas and the suburbs. The trams run from early morning until midnight, and the frequency of trams is every 10-20 minutes.

- **Bike:** Valencia is a bike-friendly city, and there are many bike rental options available. The city has a network of bike lanes that cover the entire city, making it easy and safe to bike around.

- **Taxi:** Taxis are readily available in Valencia, and they are a convenient and safe way to get around the city. Taxis can be hailed on the street, or they can be ordered by phone or through a mobile app.

- **Walking:** Valencia is a compact city, and many of its attractions are within walking distance of each other. Walking is a great way to explore the city and discover its hidden gems.

Overall, Valencia's public transportation system is reliable, affordable, and easy to use, making it an excellent choice for getting around the city.

Where to Stay in Valencia

There are many different types of accommodations available in Valencia to meet a variety of needs and interests. Here are some of Valencia's most well-liked lodging areas:

- **Old Town:** Valencia's Central Market, Cathedral, and Lonja de la Seda are all located in the Old Town, which is the city's cultural and historical centre. It offers a variety of lodging choices, including affordable hostels, five-star hotels, and flats.

- **Eixample:** Eixample is a chic and up-to-date neighbourhood in Valencia that is well-known for its designer stores, hip clubs, and eateries. A wide variety of hotels, including boutique and design hotels, are available there.

- The bohemian district of Ruzafa is a favourite among young travellers and backpackers. It features a thriving nightlife scene and a variety of affordable lodging choices, including hostels and low-cost hotels.

- **Malvarrosa Beach:** Malvarrosa Beach is a terrific place to stay if you're seeking a beach vacation. There are several residences and hotels there that have sea views.

- Many of Valencia's top museums and tourist destinations are located in the city's modern and futuristic City of Arts and Sciences neighbourhood. There are numerous hotels and apartments there, many of which are close to the museums.

Overall, Valencia has something to offer for every kind of traveller, and depending on your interests and budget, there are many great places to stay.

Staying Safe

Although Valencia is generally a safe city, it is still advisable to exercise some common sense safety measures when visiting any new place. Here are some safety recommendations for Valencia:

- Keep alert and aware of your surroundings, particularly in congested areas or at popular tourist destinations, as is important in any urban area.

- **Keep an eye on your possessions:** Petty crime, like pickpocketing, can happen in crowded places, so it's crucial to pay attention to your possessions, particularly in major tourist locations and on public transportation.

- **Hire authorised taxis:** If you need to hire a taxi, make sure that it is authorised and that you have an agreement on the fee before you get in. Asking your hotel or a local for the name of a reliable cab operator is another smart move.

- Generally speaking, it's advisable to avoid walking alone at night in any city, especially in new locations.

- Despite Valencia's reputation as a pleasant city, it is advisable to exercise caution around strangers, especially if they approach you on the street or in a bar or nightclub.

- Prepare yourself by becoming familiar with Valencia's emergency phone numbers, which include those for the police, ambulance, and fire service.

Overall, you can have a safe and enjoyable trip to Valencia by following some simple safety precautions.

USEFUL PHRASES

Here are some Spanish words and phrases you can use while visiting Valencia:

Hola - Hello

Adiós - Goodbye

Por favor - Please

Gracias - Thank you

De nada - You're welcome

Perdón - Excuse me

Lo siento - I'm sorry

¿Hablas inglés? - Do you speak English?

No entiendo - I don't understand

¿Dónde está...? - Where is...?

¿Cuánto cuesta? - How much does it cost?

La cuenta, por favor - The bill, please

¿Tienes un mapa de la ciudad? - Do you have a city map?

¿Cómo llego a...? - How do I get to...?

¿Me puede ayudar? - Can you help me?

Learning some basic Spanish phrases can help you navigate your way around Valencia and communicate with locals.

CONCLUSION

Valencia is a stunning city with a bustling culinary scene, a rich cultural history, and lots of unspoiled natural beauty. Valencia has much to offer, whether you're interested in history, art, or just unwinding on the beach.

We've selected some of the top restaurants, sightseeing attractions, and day trips and excursions from Valencia in this travel guide. Additionally, we have given you useful advice on how to reach Valencia, navigate the area, and keep yourself safe while there.

We hope this guide has motivated you to travel to Valencia and take advantage of everything this amazing city has to offer. Valencia will leave you with priceless memories whether you're travelling alone, with friends, or with family.

FINAL THOUGHTS ON VALENCIA

Valencia is a city of contrasts, fusing the new with the old, cutting-edge design with historic sites, and a buzzing cultural scene with a laid-back Mediterranean way of life. Valencia is renowned for its breathtaking coastline, delectable cuisine, and famous sights like the City of Arts and Sciences and the monuments and structures of the old town.

The internationally renowned Fallas festival and La Tomatina, which draw tourists from all over the world, are just two of the many festivals and events that take place all year long in Valencia.

Visitors can fully immerse themselves in local traditions and customs in Valencia, which is a warm and welcoming city with friendly residents. The city's many parks, gardens, and natural regions also offer opportunities for leisurely outdoor pursuits.

Whether you're interested in history, art, food, or simply soaking up the Mediterranean weather and the laid-back lifestyle, Valencia is a destination that has something for everyone.

Valencia Future in Tourism

Valencia continues to draw tourists from all over the world, therefore the city's future in tourism is promising. With a focus on sustainable tourism practices, the city has been heavily investing in promoting its cultural history, gastronomy, and natural beauty.

Valencia has also gained recognition as a top location for creativity and innovation, with the City of Arts and Sciences serving as a representation of Valencia's progressive outlook.

With a focus on cultural and gastronomic tourism, the city has been attempting to broaden its tourism offers beyond conventional sun and beach tourism. Valencia's culinary culture is particularly remarkable, with the city's chefs and restaurants winning accolades from around the world for their creative takes on classic cuisine.

Additionally, Valencia has been making investments in its infrastructure, including enlarging its airport and enhancing its public transportation system, to make it simpler for tourists to navigate and explore the city.

With a dedication to sustainable tourism practices, a wide variety of attractions, and a welcoming attitude that continues to draw tourists from all over the world, Valencia's future in the tourism industry overall appears bright.

Travel Guide To Valencia 101

Not Beer from wheatlesswanderlust.com
Sin GLUIO
Cenacos Madrid
Sana Locura (Bakery   Calle del General Oráa 43
                between Núñez de Bilbao + Avenida de America)
                     gfree line   orange (Green line
LAIB   gf bread
Grosso Napoletano   in Guten - Calle de V (Chueka)
                                   Fernado VI
Japanese curry at Okashi Sanda.
Venezuelan style Arepas at GUASA
Solo de Croquetas - Calle de Echegaray
    (Ramo de tapas) Near Anton Martin (W-M)
                                  matin
                        Calle

Restuarante Vegeteriano Artemisia Sol: 100%
Gmlerpee + veg

LAIB   Bakery

C